A Greek Primer

A GREEK PRIMER

For Beginners in New Testament Greek

μηδὲν ἄγαν

BY

WALLACE N. STEARNS

THE METHODIST BOOK CONCERN

NEW YORK   CINCINNATI

Copyright, 1914, by
WALLACE N. STEARNS

A scholarly knowledge of Greek requires some time and effort. Every preacher and teacher of the New Testament books would be greatly helped by being able even to refer to the dictionary and to pick out the critical notes in a high-grade commentary.

In many instances memory has grown dim, and there is need of some not too pretentious guide to a new beginning.

Out of many such experiences this meager outline has come, an attempt built up on the old maxim, "Do not in the beginning attempt too much."

SUGGESTIONS

1. Learn principles. Language preceded grammar, and the latter is at best a generalization of the former.

2. Learn words. Acquire a vocabulary. The first step is to know words and, further, to know them in their Greek dress.

3. Read aloud. The ear lends efficient help to the eye. There is an indefinable swing even to Greek prose that facilitates study.

4. Commit passages—however brief—to memory. Better than rules is a fund of actual examples, stored up in the memory, of Greek as it was spoken and written.

5. With this outline the text of the fourth Gospel should be used from the start (see notice on next page) for study, reading aloud, and for memorizing.

6. Remember that in the end all methods avail little. The way to do a thing is to do it.

ABBREVIATIONS USED

B. M. T.   Burton's New Testament Moods and Tenses.

Bt.   Babbit's Grammar of Attic and Ionic Greek.

G.   Gildersleeve's Syntax of Classical Greek.

Gl.   Goodell's School Grammar of Attic Greek.

G. M. T.   Goodwin's Greek Moods and Tenses.

Gn.   Goodwin's Greek Grammar.

H. A.   Hadley and Allen's Greek Grammar.

Useful beginning books are:

Huddilston's Essentials of New Testament Greek (Macmillan, 65 cents).

The Gospel of John in Greek, issued by the Massachusetts Bible Society (10 cents a copy).

Moulton's Brief Dictionary of New Testament Greek (Hinds and Noble, $1.00); or Green's Greek-English Lexicon to the New Testament (with supplement. Hastings, Boston, 75 cents).

I. THE ALPHABET

1. In learning a new alphabet attention need be paid only to such letters as are not already known. Of the Greek alphabet only twelve characters are unfamiliar:

A,	B,	Γ,	Δ,	E,	Z,	H,	Θ,	I,	K,	Λ,	M,
α,	β,	γ,	δ,	ε,	ζ,	η,	θ,	ι,	κ,	λ,	μ,
a,	b,	g,	d,	ĕ,	z,	ē,	th,	i,	k,	l,	m,

N,	Ξ,	O,	Π,	P,	Σ,	T,	Υ,	Φ,	X,	Ψ,	Ω.
ν,	ξ,	ο,	π,	ρ,	σ(ς),	τ,	υ,	φ,	χ,	ψ,	ω.
n,	ks,	ŏ,	p,	r,	s,	t,	u,	ph,	ch,	ps,	ō.

NOTE.—The small letters, most used, should be learned. The capital letters may be learned as they occur.

2. $ε$, o are always short; $η$, $ω$, always long; a, $ι$, $υ$, sometimes long, sometimes short.

ā as "a" in father. ῑ as "i" in machine.
ă as "a" in papa. ῐ as "i" in pin.
η as "e" in fete. ω as "o" in note.
ε as "e" in met. o as "o" in obey.

$υ$ equals approximately "eu" in feud or the French u.

NOTE 1.—In diphthongs with a long vowel $ι$ is subscribed.

9

NOTE 2.—As in music, the difference between *long* and *short* is one of time, as ⎯⎯. A difference in quality actually appears ⎯⎯ in pronunciation.

NOTE 3.—A diphthong is counted long. But in determining accent final –αι– and –οι– are counted short except in the optative mode and in a few words, οἴμοι, οἶκοι. Bt. 3–4; Gl. 5; Gn. 5; H. A. 9–11.

3. The consonants are classified:

(1) Mutes—

	Smooth	Middle	Rough	With s
Labial,	π	β	φ	ψ
Palatal,	κ	γ	χ	ξ
Lingual,	τ	δ	θ	ζ

(2) Liquids—

λ, μ, ν, ρ, as in English, σ(ς) is a sibilant.

(3) ζ, ξ, ψ are called double consonants. Bt. 12; Gl. 38; Gn. 18–22.

1. There are as many syllables in a word as there are separate vowels and diphthongs.

2. Consonants are pronounced with succeeding vowels: λό-γος, πο-λί-της, ἐ-λέ-γε-το. Where two consonants occur together, they are not separated at the beginning of a word or in the case of combinations that do occur at the beginnings of words. G. 97; H. A. 91.

II. ACCENT

Accent occurs on one of the last three syllables, and represents to the eye the movement of the voice in pronouncing words. Its practical value is to indicate the stress of the voice in reading.

NOTE 1.—Accent forms are three (acute ´, grave `, and circumflex ˜) and may be summarized thus:

$$
\textit{Short ultima} \left\{ \begin{array}{l} \text{antepenult ´} \\ \text{short penult ´} \\ \text{long penult ˜} \\ \text{ultima ´} \end{array} \right.
$$

$$
\textit{Long ultima} \left\{ \begin{array}{l} \text{penult ´} \\ \text{ultima ´ or ˜} \end{array} \right.
$$

NOTE 2.—In composition acute accent on the last syllable becomes grave.

NOTE 3.—Accent is often arbitrary. Rules indicate where accent *may* (not *must*) occur.

III. BREATHINGS

Words beginning with a vowel are pronounced with or without aspiration (initial "h"). Aspiration is indicated by the sign (‘), ὅτι (hoti). Unaspirated syllables are marked (’), οὐκ (ook).

American him is ‘im; horse is ‘orse.

English im is ’im; orse is ’orse.

NOTE 1.—Breathing stands over the vowel: in a

diphthong, over the second vowel (accent also stands over the second vowel, and precedes the breathing). Bt. 8; Gl. 6; Gn. 11.

Note may be made of the marks of punctuation: comma (,), colon (·), interrogation (;), period (.).

IV. DECLENSIONS

1. There are three numbers; singular, dual, and plural. In late Greek the dual is less frequent and except the numeral δύο, does not occur in the New Testament. Bt. 74; Gl. 57; Gn. 155; H. A. 123.

2. The five cases are the nominative, genitive (equals of, or a possessive), dative (equals to, for, with), accusative (equals English objective), vocative (as in direct address). Bt. 74; Gl. 59; Gn. 160; H. A. 123.

3. The o– declension (stems end in –o–).

	SING.		DUAL (rare in late Greek)	PLURAL	
	Mas.	Neut.	Mas. and Neut.	Mas.	Neut.
Nom.	–ος	–ον	–ω	–οι	–ἄ
Gen.	–ου	–ου	–οιν	–ων	–ων
Dat.	–ῳ	–ῳ	–οιν	–οις	–οις
Acc.	–ον	–ον ,	–ω	–ους	–ἄ
Voc.	–ε	–ον	–ω	–οι	–ἄ

(or same as Nom.)

    (1) Masculine nouns (and a few feminines) end in –ος in Nom. Sing.: Neuters end in –ον.

(2) The stem of an –o– noun may be found by dropping the case-ending and adding the stem vowel –o–. Bt. 76; Gl. 62; Gn. 192; H. A. 133.

EXAMPLES

Determine stem in each of the following words and affix the above case-endings. Note changes in accent and the reasons therefor. ἄρτος, στόλος, λό-γος, υἱός, ἄνθρωπος, ἱερόν; σοφός, σοφόν; αὐτός, οὗτος.

Translate and construe:

1. λέγει (says) αὐτῷ ὁ Φίλιππος. 2. ἐν τῷ τοῦ Κρό-νου ἱερῷ. 3. καλεῖται (is called) οὗτος ὁ τόπος βίος. 4. περίβολος ἦν (was), ἐν αὐτῷ ἔχων (having, = with) ἑτέρους περιβόλους δύο. 5. οὗτοι οἱ λόγοι πιστοὶ καὶ ἀληθινοί.

4. The a– declension (stems end in –a–).

	SING. Fem.	Mas.	DUAL Fem. and Mas.	PLURAL Fem. and Mas.
Nom.	–a, –η	–aς, –ης	–ā	–aι
Gen.	–āς, –ης	–ov, –ov	–aιν	–ῶν
Dat.	–ᾳ, –ῃ	–ᾳ, –ῃ	–aιν	–aις
Acc.	–aν, –ην	–aν, –ην	–ā	–āς
Voc.	–a, –η	–a, –a	–ā	–aι

(1) Feminine nouns in the Nom. Sing. end in –ă, –ā, or –η; mas. nouns, in –aς or –ης.

(2) In the gen. sing., mas. nouns end in –ov.

(3) Except in the genitive, final –a in the sing.

is short when not preceded by ε, ι, or ρ, otherwise long.

(4) If in the mas. the –ος is preceded by ε, ι,
or ρ (note 3), the fem. sing. nom. ends in
–ᾱ, otherwise in –η. Bt. 76; Gl. 66; Gn. 171;
H. A. 132–3.

EXAMPLES—AS IN 1

μοῦσα, οἰκία, χώρα, τιμή; ὁπλίτης, ταμίας; αὐτή, αὕτη;
ἡ ὁδός.

Translate and construe:

1. ἐν ἀρχῇ ἦν ὁ λόγος, καὶ ὁ λόγος ἦν πρὸς τὸν θεόν.
2. καὶ αὕτη ἐστὶν (is) ἡ μαρτυρία τοῦ 'Ιωάννου. 3. τὸ
δὲ κέντρον τοῦ θανάτου ἡ μαρτυρία. 4. ὁ στέφανος τῆς
ζωῆς. 5. ἡ πύλη τοῦ πρώτου περιβόλου. 6. Τύχη ἐστι
δὲ οὐ μόνον τυφλή, ἀλλὰ καὶ κωφή. 7. Πλάνος καὶ
῎Αγνοια.

5. The Consonant declension (stems end in a
consonant). With these are grouped in the grammar (3d declension) nouns with stems in ι, ν, or a
diphthong.

	SING.		DUAL (rare in late Greek)	PLURAL	
	Mas. and Fem.	Neut.	Mas., Fem., and Neut.	Mas. and Fem.	Neut.
Nom.	–ς or –	–	–ε	–ες	–ᾰ
Gen.	–ος	–ος	–οιν	–ων	–ων
Dat.	—ι	–ι	–οιν	–σι	–σι
Acc.	–ν or –ᾰ	–	–ε	–νς or –ᾰς	–ᾰ
Voc.	–ς or –	–	–ε	–ες	–ᾰ

(1) Necessary here is the table of mutes and their forms when combined with –s. (I, 3, 1.)

(2) All three genders occur in this declension.

(3) In gen. plural of monosyllabic nouns (as in –a– nouns) the accent is –ῶν: in datives dual and plural of tones we have –αῖν, –οῖν, –αῖς, and –οῖς. Bt. 76; Gl. 98; Gn. 225; H. A. 132–3.

Examples—as in 1

θήρ (stem θερ–), σῶμα (–τος), πίναξ (–κος), σάλπιγξ (–γγος), λαίλαψ (–πος), φλέψ (–βός), θρίξ (τριχός).

Translate and construe:

1. ἦν τὸ φῶς τὸ ἀληθινόν. 2. ἡ δύναμις τῆς ἁμαρτίας ὁ νόμος ἐστίν (is). 3. καὶ ὁ λόγος σάρξ ἐγένετο (became). 4. ἦν πίναξ ἔμπροσθεν τοῦ ναοῦ. 5. ἡ Ἀφροσύνη τοῖς ἀνθρώποις Σφίγξ ἐστιν. 6. οὕτως ἐστὶν ἡ ἀνάστασις τῶν νεκρῶν.

6. These case-endings hold for all (except indeclinables which undergo no changes) substantives, adjectives (including the definite article), pronouns, and participles (see verbs). E. g.:

	RELATIVE PRONOUNS			DEFINITE ARTICLE		
Sing.	Mas.	Fem.	Neut.	Mas.	Fem.	Neut.
Nom.	ὅς	ἥ	ὅ	ὁ	ἡ	τό
Gen.	οὗ	ἧς	οὗ	τοῦ	τῆς	τοῦ
Dat.	ᾧ	ᾗ	ᾧ	τῷ	τῇ	τῷ
Acc.	ὅν	ἥν	ὅ	τόν	τήν	τό
		etc.			etc.	

Bt. 144–9; Gl. 214; Gn. 421; H. A. 272–5.

The personal pronouns, as in other languages, are more irregular, the several parts being traceable to different stems.

	FIRST PERSON, I		SECOND PERSON, THOU	
	Sing.	Plural	Sing.	Plural
Nom.	ἐγώ	ἡ‑μεῖς	σύ	ὑ‑μεῖς
Gen.	ἐ‑μοῦ	ἡ‑μῶν	σοῦ	ὑ‑μῶν
Dat.	ἐ‑μοί	ἡ‑μῖν	σοί	ὑ‑μῖν·
Acc.	ἐ‑μέ	ἡ‑μᾶς	σέ	ὑ‑μάς

Bt. 139; Gl. 194; Gn. 389; H. A. 261.

Translate and construe:

1. ὁ προφήτης εἶ (art). 2. σὺ πίστιν ἔχεις (hast) καὶ ἐγὼ ἔργα. 3. ἐγὼ φωνὴ βοῶντος (one crying) ἐν τῇ ἐρήμῳ.

V. THE VERB: CONJUGATION

1. In the study of the verb four points are to be considered: stem; tense-signs; theme vowels (short in indicative, imperative, infinitive, and participial modes; long in the subjunctive and merged in a diphthong in the optative); and personal endings.

2. The stem is the basic part of the inflected word. To this are appended the various signs, as above, which in verb analysis must again be cut off. E. g., τι‑μά‑ω, I honor, stem τιμά. Bt. 157–61; Gl. 248; Gn. 404–7, 153; H. A. 153.

3. The tenses of the verb are called primary or secondary as they have to do with present (or

future) or past time. Taking the verb λύω as a model we have:

Primary	Secondary
Present, stem λυ–	Imperfect, stem ἐ–λυ
Future, stem λυσ–	Aorist, stem ἐ–λὺς
Perfect, stem λε–λυκ–	Pluperfect, stem ἐ–λε–λυκ
Future perfect, stem λε–λυσ	

Bt. 162; Gl. 311; Gn. 717; H. A. 372.

4. The future tenses (future, future perfect) are indicated by a σ($+$°/$ε$) appended to the stem, as λύ–ω, λύ, σω, λε–λύ–σ–ο–μαι, λύ–θή–σ–ο–ο–μαι. Bt. 212; Gn. 662; Gl. 277; H. A. 372.

5. The perfect tenses (perfect, future perfect, pluperfect) are indicated by (1) the doubling of the stem (i. e., repeating the initial consonant with ε–), and (2) in the active voice by an affixed –κ– (cf. Latin –v–). E. g., λύ–ω perf. λέ–λυ–κα (for λύ–λυ–κα).

NOTE 1.—If the verb begins with a middle or rough mute, the reduplication occurs with the corresponding smooth mute (cf. I, 3). E. g., πέ–φυ–κα (for φέ–φυ–κα). Bt. 162; Gl. 287; Gn. 455; H. A. 300–3.

6. Secondary tenses are indicated generally by the prefix ἐ–, e. g., ἐ–λυ–ο–ν, ἐ–λε–λύ–κ–ε–μεν. In case the verb itself begins with a vowel, the initial vowel is lengthened. E. g., ἀ–κού–ω, ἤ–κου–ο–ν. Bt. 171-2; Gl. 264, 293; Gn. 465, 3; H. A. 354-7.

7. The theme vowel immediately follows the

stem. In the indicative it is –o– before μ and ν, otherwise –ε–; in the subjunctive, –ω– or –η–; in the optative (mode vowel), –οι– or –αι– (aorist passive indicative, –ει–). E. g., ἔ-λυ-ο-ν, ἔ-λυ-ε-ς, λύ-ω-μαι, λύ-η-ται, λυ-οί-μην, λυ-σαί-μην. Bt. 159–60; Gl. 294–5; Gn. 568, 719, 730; H. A. 372.

(1) In aorist tenses except second aorist and aorist passive, the theme vowel is –a–.

(2) In the perfect active the theme vowel is –a–, in the pluperfect active it is –ε–.

(3) In the pluperfect middle and passive the theme vowel is omitted. E. g., λε-λύ-σ-α-μεν, λε-λύ-κ-α-τε, ἐ-λε-λύ-κ-ε-μεν, λέ-λυ-μαι, ἐ-λε-λύ-μην. Bt. 201, 222–4; Gl. 279, 288–9, 298; Gn. 669, 682–3, 698; H. A. 428, 446, 459, 461–3.

8. The sign of the passive voice is often –θε–, sometimes lengthened to –θη– in conjugation, e. g., λυ-θή-σ-ο-μαι. Bt. 231–2; Gl. 302; Gn. 707; H. A. 468.

9. The person of the verb is indicated by a letter or syllable (in origin a personal pronoun) added to end of verb. E. g., λύ-ο-μαι, ἔ-λυ-ο-ν.

10. The middle and passive voices are alike except in two tenses, the future and the aorist. Bt. 167; Gl. 263; Gn. 552; H. A. 376–80.

11. There are two sets (or double sets) of personal endings; one set for the active (primary and secondary) tenses, and one for the tenses of the

middle and passive (except second aorist and aorist passive). Bt. 166; Gl. 263, 271; Gn. 551–3; H. A. 375.

12. The personal endings may be shown thus:

Primary Tenses

Sing.	$-\omega$	$-\mu\alpha\iota$
	$-\epsilon\iota\varsigma$	$-\sigma\alpha\iota$
	$-\epsilon\iota$	$-\tau\alpha\iota$
Dual	$-\tau o\nu$	$-\sigma\theta o\nu$
	$-\tau o\nu$	$-\sigma\theta\eta\nu$
Plur.	$-\mu\epsilon\nu$	$-\mu\epsilon\theta\alpha$
	$-\tau\epsilon$	$-\sigma\theta\epsilon$
	$-o\upsilon\sigma\iota(\nu)$	$-\nu\tau\alpha\iota$

Secondary Tenses

Sing.	$-\nu$	$-\mu\eta\nu$
	$-\varsigma$	$-\sigma o$
	$- -$	$-\tau o$
Dual	$-\tau o\nu$	$-\sigma\theta o\nu$
	$-\tau\eta\nu$	$-\sigma\theta\eta\nu$
Plur.	$-\mu\epsilon\nu$	$-\mu\epsilon\theta\alpha$
	$-\tau\epsilon$	$-\sigma\theta\epsilon$
	$-\nu$	$-\nu\tau o$

(1) The longer, softer endings generally indicate middle or passive voice.

(2) In verbs as in nouns the dual is less frequent in later Greek.

13. The endings of the active participle to indicate gender are respectively $-\omega\nu$, $-o\upsilon\sigma\alpha$, $-o\nu$. The form $-o\upsilon\sigma\alpha$ is of the first declension; the others ($-o\nu\tau$, Gn. 25; Gl. 119) are of the third.

14. Middle participles are of the first and second declensions and may be recognized by the syllable $-\mu\varepsilon\nu-$. E. g., $\lambda\upsilon-\acute{o}-\mu\varepsilon\nu-o\varsigma$.

15. The active infinitive regularly ends in $-\varepsilon\iota\nu$ ($-\varepsilon\nu +$ theme vowel $-\varepsilon-$, contracted, $-\varepsilon\iota\nu$). E. g., $\lambda\acute{\upsilon}-\varepsilon\iota\nu$ (for $\lambda\upsilon-\varepsilon-\varepsilon\nu$). The passive and middle (i. e., when used as passives) infinitives regularly end in $-\sigma\theta\alpha\iota$. E. g., $\lambda\acute{\upsilon}-\varepsilon-\sigma\theta\alpha\iota$, $\lambda\acute{\upsilon}-\sigma-\alpha-\sigma\theta\alpha\iota$. The aorist passive infinitive ends in $-\nu\alpha\iota$. E. g., $\lambda\upsilon-\theta\tilde{\eta}-\nu\alpha\iota$. Bt. 167; Gl. 162, 273, 275; Gn. 301, 334.

16. Variations from the regular forms occur in the endings of the imperative:

		Active	Middle and Passive
Sing.	2.	$-$, aorist $-\nu$ ($-\theta\iota$, $-\varsigma$)	$-\sigma o$ aorist $-\alpha\iota$
		(contracts with con. vowel ιo $-o\nu$)	
	3.	$-\tau\omega$	$-\sigma\theta\omega$
Dual	2.	$-\tau o\nu$	$-\sigma\theta o\nu$
	3.	$-\tau\omega\nu$	$-\sigma\theta\omega\nu$
Plur.	2.	$-\tau\varepsilon$	$-\sigma\theta\varepsilon$
	3.	$-\nu\tau\omega\nu$ (or $\tau\omega\sigma\alpha\nu$)	$-\sigma\theta\omega\nu$ (or $-\sigma\theta\omega\sigma\alpha\nu$)

Bt. 167; Gl. 270-2; Gn. 746; H. A. 376.

17. The principal parts of the verb (which should be memorized) are the first person singular of the

active indicative present, future, first aorist, and perfect; the middle perfect; and the passive aorist. Bt. 162-3; Gl. 311; Gn. 462-5; H. A. 304c.

18. A small class of verbs (about equal to the number of irregular verbs in English) retain the more primitive personal endings (e. g., act. ind. pres. sing., -μι, -σι, -τι, remains of old pronominal forms). Of such are τί-θη-μι, δί-δω-μι, ἵ-στη-μι. Bt. 251-8; Gl. 372-4; Gn. 500-509; H. A. 476-92.

19. Certain verbs with vowel stems, as τιμά-ω, φιλέ-ω, δηλό-ω, by contraction with initial vowels in the personal endings assume forms not found in the regular verb paradigms. E. g., τιμά-εις, τίμᾶς; ἐ-τίμα-ε, ἐτίμα; ἐ-τίμα-ο-ν, ἐ-τίμων. Bt. 248-50; Gl. 313-15; Gn. 492-94; H. A. 337-41. For changes in accent see: Bt. 65; Gl. 29; Gn. 117; H. A. 37-39.

(1) These forms are best studied as they occur by reference to the grammars.

VI. SEQUENCE

1. It is a principle in Greek, as in other languages, that a certain relation must hold between the verbs of dependent clauses and those of the independent clauses on which they are based.

2. In Latin the sequence is one of tenses, primary tenses depending on primary tenses and secondary tenses on secondary tenses. But in Greek the

tenses of the dependent modes do not, in general, express distinctions of time. G. M. T. 785, 20.

3. In Greek the subjunctive in dependent clauses is treated (usually) as though it were a *primary* mode: the optative as though it were a *secondary* mode. E. g.:

τοῦτο πράττει ἵνα καλῶς ἔχῃ
τοῦτο ἔπραττε ἵνα καλῶς ἔχοι

But in the Greek of the New Testament (B. M. T. 174, 259, 344) and in Latin (Hale and Buck's Latin Grammar, 459) there is no optative in use, and the above distinction in modes no longer exists. Bt. 517, 2; Gl. 662; Gn. 448, 1249, 1267; H. A. 876. The trend of sequence is from the primary tenses of the indicative through subjunctive and optative in that order to the past tenses of the indicative. See under VII.

VII. THE CONDITIONAL SENTENCE

1. A conditional sentence is one that assumes what may or may not be true (in reality), and bases on it some other statement (i. e., the supposition is assumed to be true). Bt. 600–1; Gl. 645; Gn. 1381; H. A. 889.

2. A simple supposition implying nothing as to fulfillment, has the indicative (or an equivalent; Bt. 602, notes) in both clauses.

(1) If a specific sequence is made in present

time, then the present indicative stands in both
clauses. If in past time, a past indicative occurs
in both clauses. E. g.:

Present εἰ τοῦτο πράττει, καλῶς ἔχει.
Past   εἰ τοῦτο ἔπραττε, καλῶς εἶχε.

NOTE 1.—The same tense need not necessarily
stand in both clauses, e. g., εἰ τοῦτο ἔπραττε, καλῶς
ἔχει.

(2) A general reference if in present time, expressing a customary or repeated action or a general
truth, has ἐάν with the subjunctive in the if-clause
and in the conclusion the present indicative or
some form denoting present repetition, e. g., ἐὰν
τοῦτο ποιῇ, καλῶς ἔχει. If the supposition is in the
past time, the if-clause will have the optative with
εἰ and in the conclusion will stand the imperfect
indicative or some form denoting past repetition,
e. g., εἰ τοῦτο πράττοι, καλῶς εἶχε. Bt. 608–10; Gl.
651; Gn. 1393; H. A. 890, 892–4.

3. The supposition may imply something as to
the likelihood of fulfillment.

(1) If fulfillment is likely (and such contingencies
are related to future time), then the if-clause will
have ἐάν with the subjunctive and a future indicative (or an equivalent) will stand in the conclusion. This form is styled "future vivid." E. g.,
ἐὰν τοῦτο πράττῃ, καλῶς ἔξοι. If fulfillment is less
than likely ("future less vivid"), εἰ with the opta-

tive will stand in the if-clause, the optative with ἄν (potential optative) in the conclusion. E. g., εἰ τοῦτο πράττοι καλῶς ἄν ἔχοι. Bt. 604–5; Gl. 650–1; Gn. 1403.

(2) A supposition contrary to fact has in the if-clause εἰ with a past indicative; in the conclusion, a past indicative with ἄν (potential indicative). E. g., εἰ τοῦτο ἔπραττε, καλῶς ἄν εἶχε. Bt. 606; Gl. 649; Gn. 13197; H. A. 895.

NOTE 1.—For summary of conditional sentences, see Bt. 611; Gl. 645; Gn. 1387; H. A. 891.

VIII. FINAL CLAUSES

1. Pure final clauses (expressing purpose or motive) take the subjunctive when dependent on primary tenses, the optative when dependent on secondary tenses. The conjunction is ἵνα, ὡς, or ὅπως. E. g.,

> τοῦτο πράττει ἵνα καλῶς ἔχῃ.
> τοῦτο ἔπραττε ἵνα καλῶς ἔχοι

Bt. 590; Gl. 640; Gn. 365; H. A. 881.

2. Object clauses dependent on verbs denoting care, attention or effort, regularly take the future indicative ὅπως, though the future optative is possible when dependent on a secondary tense. E. g.,

> φροντίζει ὅπως καλῶς ἔξει,
> ἐφρόντιζεν ὅπας καλῶς ἔζει (or ἔζοι, see note).

Bt. 593; Gn. 1872; H. A. 885.

3. Subordinate clauses introduced by μή (trans. *lest* or *that*), and dependent on verbs denoting fear, caution or danger, take the subjunctive when dependent on primary tenses, the optative when dependent on secondary tenses. E. g.,

φοβεῖται μὴ τοῦτο πράττωμεν

ἐφοβεῖτο μὴ τοῦτο πράττοιμεν (or πράττωμεν, see note).

Bt. 593; Gl. 610; Gn. 1378.

NOTE 1.—In rules 1–3, for greater vividness—as though using the language of the person who conceived the purpose—the subjunctive may be used even when dependent on a secondary tense (see examples above). Gl. 638; Gn. 1372.

IX. INDIRECT DISCOURSE

1. A statement or question of a speaker or writer may be quoted directly, i. e., without change in the form of the language. E. g.:

Direct: τοῦτο πράξω

Indirect: λέγει

   or ὅτι τοῦτο πράξει.

   ἔλεγε

Bt. 668; Gl. 623; Gn. 1475.

2. Or it may be a change to adapt it to the form of the sentence of which it becomes a part. The form of change will depend on the introductory verb of saying, φημί, λέγω, or εἶπον.

(1) If φημί, the main verb of the quotation will be changed to the infinitive mode of the same tense and voice. E. g.:

> Direct: τοῦτο πράττω
> Indirect: φησί
> or { τοῦτο πράττειν.
> ἔφη

(2) If λέγω with ὅτι or ὡς, no change will occur when dependent on a primary tense. When dependent on a secondary tense, indicatives and subjunctives *may* (not *must*) be changed to corresponding tenses (and voice) of the optative; optatives will remain unchanged. E. g.:

> Direct: τοῦτο πράξω
> Indirect: { λέγει ὅτι τοῦτο πράξει
>   { ἔλεγε ὅτι τοῦτο πράξει (or πράξοι).

(1) Note the change *in person* to indicate the change of *speaker.*

(2) εἶπον as a verb of saying *requires*, and λέγω in the active voice *prefers* the ὅτι (ὡς) construction.

(3) Where changes of mode might occasion doubt as to the form of the original direct discourse, no changes are made. E. g., the imperfect or pluperfect indicative with ἄν, the potential optative with ἄν, or the aorist indicative in a subordinate clause (cf. Bt. 675). Bt. 678; Gl. 624; Gn. 1523; 1481, 1497.

CPSIA information can be obtained
at www.ICGtesting.com
Printed in the USA
LVHW08s1442240918
591186LV00012B/520/P